Color Your C
GREAT FLOWER PAINTINGS

Rendered by
MARTY NOBLE

DOVER PUBLICATIONS, INC.
Mineola, New York

NOTE

In the sixteenth and seventeenth centuries, the cultivation of flower gardens became popular in Italy and the Netherlands. The Dutch collected rare flowers, sometimes paying extravagant amounts for a single bulb. Naturally, they also paid special interest to the art of flower painting, and many of the greatest floral works, produced by such masters of the period as Ambrosius Bosschaert and Jan van Huysum, remain unsurpassed.

In the nineteenth century, the French Impressionists found in flower painting an ideal medium for expressing light and its effect on color, Édouard Manet and Claude Monet being perhaps the leading practitioners of the art. Post-impressionists such as Vincent van Gogh created their own vibrant approach to color that was particularly well suited to flower painting.

This collection, rendered by artist Marty Noble, traces the development of floral painting from the Dutch masters of the 1600s to the celebrated artists of the early twentieth century. All thirty of the floral paintings in this book are shown in full color on the inside front and back covers. Use this color scheme as a guide to create your own adaptation or change the colors to see the effects of color and tone on each painting.

Bibliographical Note

Color Your Own Great Flower Paintings is a new work, first published by Dover Publications, Inc., in 2004.

DOVER *Pictorial Archive* SERIES

This book belongs to the Dover Pictorial Archive Series. You may use the designs and illustrations for graphics and crafts applications, free and without special permission, provided that you include no more than four in the same publication or project. (For permission for additional use, please write to Permissions Department, Dover Publications, Inc., 31 East 2nd Street, Mineola, N.Y. 11501.)

However, republication or reproduction of any illustration by any other graphic service, whether it be in a book or in any other design resource, is strictly prohibited.

International Standard Book Number: 0-486-43335-8

Manufactured in the United States of America
Dover Publications, Inc., 31 East 2nd Street, Mineola, N.Y. 11501

1. Jacob Marrel (1614–1681). *Flower Piece.* 1647. Oil on panel.

2. Jan Van Kessel (1626–1679). *A Vase of Flowers.* 1600s. Oil on panel.

3. **Jan Battista van Fornenburgh** (*fl.* 1608–1649). *Bouquet in a Roemer.*

4. **Ambrosius Bosschaert** (1573–1621). *Flowers in a Glass Vase.* 1614. Oil on copper.

5. Ambrosius Bosschaert (1573–1621). *Bouquet of Flowers on a Ledge.* Ca. 1619. Oil on panel.

6. **Giovanna Garzoni** (1600–1670). *Flowers in a Glass Vase.* 1600s.

7. Giovanna Garzoni (1600–1670). *Flowers in a Chinese Vase with Fig and Bean.* 1600s. Gouache and black pencil on parchment.

8. Jan van Huysum (1682–1749). *Flower Piece.*

9. **Jan van Huysum** (1682–1749). *Hollyhocks and Other Flowers in a Vase.* 1702. Oil on canvas.

10. Anne Vallayer-Coster (1744–1818). *Flowers in a Blue Vase.* 1782. Oil on canvas.

11. Severin Roesen (ca. 1815–1872). *Still Life: Flowers and Fruit* (detail). 1850–55.

12. Claude Monet (1840–1926). *Spring Flowers*. 1864. Oil on canvas.

13. Frédéric Bazille (1841–1870). *Flowers.* 1868. Oil on canvas.

14. Édouard Manet (1832–1883). *Peonies in a Vase on a Stand.* 1864. Oil on canvas.

15. Édouard Manet (1832–1883). *Lilac and Roses in a Little Glass Vase.* 1882. Oil on canvas.

16. **Pierre-Auguste Renoir** (1841–1919). *Spring Bouquet.* 1866. Oil on canvas.

17. Pierre-Auguste Renoir (1841–1919). *Mixed Flowers in an Earthenware Pot.* 1869. Oil on canvas.

18. Pierre-Auguste Renoir (1841–1919). *Roses in a Vase.* Ca. 1909.

19. Camille Pissarro (1830–1903). *Chrysanthemums in a Chinese Vase.* 1873. Oil on canvas.

20. George Cochran Lambdin (1830–1896). *Flowers in a Vase.* 1875.

21. Paul Cézanne (1839–1906). *Blue Vase.* 1883–87.

22. Berthe Morisot (1841–1905). *Dahlias*. Ca. 1876. Oil on canvas.

23. Vincent van Gogh (1853–1890). *Majolica Jar with Branches of Oleander.* 1888. Oil on canvas.

24. Vincent van Gogh (1853–1890). *Sunflowers.* 1888. Oil on canvas.

25. Vincent van Gogh (1853–1890). *Vase with Violet Irises against a Yellow Background.*
1890. Oil on canvas.

26. Paul Gauguin (1848–1903). *Still Life with Flowers.* 1891.

27. Katherine Cameron (1874–1968). *Still Life with Roses in a Glass.* 1894. Watercolor on paper.

28. Odilon Redon (1840–1916). *Wildflowers.* Ca. 1905. Pastel.

29. Henri Rousseau (1844–1910). *Flowers in a Vase.* 1909. Oil on canvas.

30. Pierre Bonnard (1867–1947). *Bouquet of Flowers.*